Always Together

A Collection of Poetry by
Laura Chagnon

Copyright © Civin Media Relations

All Rights Reserved. No part of this publication may be reproduced, stored in a retrieval system or transmitted in any form by any means electronic, mechanical, or photocopying, recording or otherwise without permission in writing from the author.

Request for permission to make copies of any part of the work should be submitted online to todd@civinmediarelations.com

ISBN: 979834408781

Imprint: Independently published

Published by Civin Media Relations

www.civinmediarelations.com

Printed in the United States

Dedication

I lovingly dedicate this book to God. He saved my life and to Him goes all the glory.

To my parents Wayne and Carole ~Your love and support during all these years is appreciated more than you can ever imagine.

Pastor Jack and Tammy ~ Your faith and love has guided my ship. I am so grateful for our friendship.

My wonderful friend, Todd Civin ~ This is book number twelve. What an incredible journey. I love you.

Jennifer ~ Such a sweet angel. You played such a key role in publishing this book. You are heaven-sent.

Tom, my partner in life ~You carry me through peaceful waters. Our love always reaching new heights.

Always Together
Poems by Laura Chagnon

April	6
Faith	7
Only A Whisper Away	8
A Raven In Moonlight	9
Spellbound	10
The Cradle of Spring	11
Music of the World	12
How Many Ways Can I Write About Happiness?	13
Spirit of Winter	14
Sparrows	15
Winter's Child	16
Home	17
Addicted	18
Lost Faith	19
Perennial	20
Rising Sun	21
Meadows	22
Afraid to Die	23
Snow Angels	24
Human Nature	25
Dark Butterfly	26
Feeling the Wind	27
The Rising	28
Gratitude	29
The First Rose	30

A Tribute to Our Father	31
Wild Violets	32
The Truth about This Hour	33
Goodbye	34
A Conversation with an August Night	35
Always Together	36
My Brothers	37
My Two Angels RyRy and Sandy Madden	38
My Onyx Friends	39
Writing Angels	40
Barefoot in Heaven	41
The Heart of Summer	42
Kind People	43
In the Present Moment	44
More Than a Job	45
About the Author	46

~April~

*She wears a blue bonnet
tied loosely on her head
and has been here
since the beginning of time.
Everything about her, delicious,
newborn flowers, delicate.
She is that one bird whose
crystal peep is more than a sound,
more than a song.
Of course it is paradise,
how could it not be?
And if your hands ache
for something to do,
remove the sky's top hat,
gather the clouds,
the sun, the moon
and the stars at twilight—
Gather them close,
and feel hope's message,
grateful in your soul.*

~ Faith~

Sometimes in this life

the sky seems to be

peering through hazel eyes

and the clouds in our horizon

filled with snow,

and we wonder

where is the sun?

Never be afraid because

God's light is always shining

on his children.

Let faith forever be

the blossom in your garden.

When you step outside,

feel the glow from heaven

and understand the truth --

the truth --

you are never alone.

~Only A Whisper Away~

The clock is ticking
in the hearts of cicadas,
the shadows of time moving fast.

The core of summer, molten lava,
my heart captured in your tender fire.

Dear Cicadas, all day I listen
to the rise and fall
of your romantic call,

I hear your phantom tymbals calling,
your passion trembling in the season
of dreams.

And I am twilight,
visiting summer's splendor,
listening to your last symphony,

as the hand of darkness
draws the velvet curtain
to my lips for your final kiss.

I am the wilting petals of a rose,
as I hear your song resonating in
the August wind--

for I know your silence is
only a whisper away.

~A Raven in Moonlight~

Our noble earth alive again
The flowers and the squirrels,
Pink blossoms of the Dogwood,
I love their fancy curls.

White frosted clouds are drifting
In a light blue porcelain sky,
Pinch me, am I dreaming
For I can't believe my eyes.

I watch a monarch posing
Upon a blade of grass,
Each flower, tree and butterfly
Perform in earth's sweet dance.

The sun a golden candle
Burns longer in the day,
As birds chatter gaily
They have so much to say.

Spring days sweet and new
Kissed by the wand of sun,
Leaf sounds moving in the wind
Delivering heaven's song.

Through the window of my room
Twilight, my dear friend,
Blessing earth with color
As the day comes to an end.

And from his nest of darkness
My beloved Raven flies,
His silken black wings shimmer
In the star-filled, moonlit sky.

~Spellbound~

*The box that was your home
all winter, small
overnight transformed--a paradise
without walls, without ceilings
where miracles begin.*

*In the hand of fairies, a wand,
changing reality into dreams,*

*and somewhere in the night, a song,
the most breathtaking voice,
whispers, whispers in your ear.*

Just open your eyes and believe.

~The Cradle of Spring~

I look through the window
At the buds on the trees,
Everything's waking
There's so much to see.

There's a nest in the maple
Of blue speckled eggs,
On the ground newborn creatures
With four furry legs.

I see scampering chipmunks
And squirrels on the wire,
Filling my heart
With springtime desire.

Four newborn ducklings
Crossing the road,
In my backyard pond
That old friendly toad.

The sun earned her wings
Perching high in the sky,
In company with birds
And their sweet lullaby.

I gaze at the stars
At the crimson of twilight, God's
pefect creation
A miraculous sight.

I look through the window
At the buds on the trees,
Everything's waking
There's so much to see.

~Music of the World~

All the birds are back
Singing their song,
In the company of angels
How could anything be
wrong?

A ballad so charming
Drifts through the air,
On wind from the heavens
Through flowers so fair.

God's musicians performing
As tree limbs sway,
Their beautiful symphony
Takes me so far away.

A mural of blue sky
As far as I can see,
The melody of sparrows
Sets my spirit free.

Each day of May
A most glorious time,
The morning dove's coo
In harmonious rhyme.

Each bird is so precious
A blessing from God,
Their song in the wind
As flower heads nod.

From my window I hear them
Through the sky's blue swirl,
Serenading spirits
All across the world.

~How Many Ways Can I Write About Happiness?~

In the delightful months of spring and summer,
to write about happiness, the ways are endless.
For doesn't it seem to be waiting around every corner?

It begins in the heavens as God lowers the sun,
warming the days with the blessings of hope.

The blue of sky, a gallery, exhibiting clouds
a pure white perfection--a paradise where angels
flaunt their wings.

And behold, the music-- the symphony,
the privilege every day

to be amidst the harmony of birds.

It begins in the heavens as God lowers the sun,
warming the days with the blessings of hope--

And simply for the gift of life
which sets my feet to dancing.

~Spirit of Winter~

*On the threshold of winter, November's wind, a tempest
ravaging autumn's trees—the limbs stripped to bare bones.*

*In the snowy hills and pastures a white stallion,
unpredictable, kicking up his wild hooves.*

*And there she is—spirit of winter, breathtaking.
As far as the eye can see, page upon page,
an eternity of glistening snow.*

*White fields, barren trees, crystal castles,
snow falling from charcoal skies a masterpiece of elegance.*

~Sparrows~

For as long as I can remember
The sparrows, my dearest friends,
When I was born, my shell cracked,
And it was their nest that I was in.

Dancing through the seasons
They frolic all year long,
And my darling precious angels
Fill the air with song.

I love their joyful faces
Petite, and charming ways,
Such delightful musicians
I wake to every day.

Look closely at the sparrows
And see what I adore,
Watch their playful antics
In the blue skies as they soar.

And so my dearest friends
This tribute just for you,
As I listen to your fading songs
As twilight bids adieu.

~Winter's Child~

*As the last leaf falls from the temple of autumn,
the curtain opens to a new season.
Pillars of trees stand noble and bare.
Mother Earth eagerly awaits winter's child to join her.*

*Like an arrow, tall and regal pine trees
pierce the satin sky, and beneath the clouds of snow,
here comes cardinal with her delicate grace,
darting here, darting there, trimming the trees with
ruby ribbons, the essence of her joy.*

~Home~

In suffering arms, anguish carries him through rivers of fear.
Becoming the animal, pacing nervously in the tiny space he has left,
that cubical with one bed and one chair.

He becomes blind to the gentleman in the next bed and deaf
to the cries in the night.
His breath is still as he lingers in a garden of isolated souls.

There are no words left as he crawls inside his closet cave.
Every day his grave gets deeper.

The gray skies look hopeless as the snow begins
to fall upon the frozen ground.
The crow, perched on a jagged branch, looks ahead into destiny.
To the Angels his urgent spirit whispers, "Please let me in."

~Addicted~

Where you are today,
I was that spider
Weaving the tedious web,
Alone, entangled in fear.

My mind was small,
Crawling through
All those narrow alleys,
Grasping for strength,
Reaching out,
Holding onto the tornado
Through all those dark years.

They saw my devastation
And felt me disappear.
I was blind to their concern,
Keeping my distance.

I was where you are,
In pain,
Scuttling through the night,
Trapped beneath a liar's moon.

~Lost Faith~

Along back roads

He walks through ruins of sin,

Feet bloodied, lost faith.

I see his face defeated

with broken promises.

I walk to the sacred hill

Where a flower still grows,

Petal soft--the face of Jesus

Before the last betrayal.

~ *Perennial*~

Don't think of these things anymore

    Sweet daffodil in the sky

    The gentle blush of rose

    The sound of frog and crickets.

Oh, dearest lover, warm yellow kite, dying every year,

I'll pull you down myself with autumn's curtain

So trees can get undressed.

Shed no tears for summer,

    Short visit from a distant aunt,

You taught me how to grieve.

~ Rising Sun ~

I wake to a voice that only I can hear.

It is the swan gliding soundless on the lake.

It is the quiet bird in meditation.

It is the beginning of life, the spark of hope.

You pulled the covers back from night.

I hear your voice yearning to awaken,

The urgent whisper through dreams.

~Meadows~

I am bound to this muddied world of devastation.

My mortal flesh holds me here, but I am forgiven.

I am a butterfly breaking through the clouds,

Sympathizing with the world I left behind.

Beyond the clouds, a place of wild flowers

growing in green meadows.

A place of where all butterflies are free.

~Afraid to Die~

*She feels dark hands upon her,
more bones than flesh.*

*She listens to the earth's belabored breath.
A tree stands in the yard,
withered arms, outstretched and brittle,
the darkness swallows it whole.*

*White, crater eyes wrinkle.
The owl is nestled in her arms,
her only warmth.*

*She envies the living,
their easy motions
going through each day.*

*When the owl moves,
the wind groans,
her spirit cries.*

*She accepts the loneliness;
she accepts the owl's heart
beating in her hand.*

*She has slept so long
beneath the leaves,
alone in the dark.*

*Her mortal soul recoils
remaining in the earth.*

~ *Snow Angels* ~

*Listen to the birds' frantic ballads,
their songs a grand finale,
before the wind beckons them south.*

*The shadows are pulling together,
draping the sun with early death.*

*The ground becomes a frozen tomb,
skeletons dance in the moonlight
as the wind rattles through naked branches.*

*Clouds open up,
a purse dropping silver coins,
like angels falling from the dark sky.*

*Their tiny wings join together,
creating a diamond quilt
that sparkles in the early morning sun.*

Their lonely song echoes in the frozen silence.

~ *Human Nature* ~

Night is where the owl lives,
wrapped in evening air.
Eyes, large and blinking,
like seconds of time,
time that escapes into space.

Birds fly through clouds,
their freedom is admired.

Jet planes, man's invention,
and idea we borrowed.

Imagine a world without wings.
If time stood still,
our heads would fall off
and roll under trees.

Dark angels of night,
the owl would recognize
our insatiable hearts,
threading its nest with our hair,
picking at flesh
and eating our souls
to fill their hunger.

We would shudder inside and whisper,
"How cruel. We are one of them now."

Blinded by passion
that is our blood.
Our desire to conquer
is a sign of our undoing.

Our eyes look skyward into silence,
and the only thing left is time.

~Dark Butterfly~

Water is ice
    tears freeze to my cheeks.
The sun dips its ladle in the sky
    already dark.

Cold flowers
    dark butterfly wings
    flutter to nowhere.

When even the crimson of twilight is lost
    the black cape of reality
    peers through my window.

~Feeling the Wind~

There is a poem in her soul, thoughts in her eyes.

She is a ray of rising sun, a bird feeling the wind,

an obsession far away from the world, a buried dream

of night, a spirit in the walls. If she breaks the glass

too soon, the moon will slip through a hole in a sky

without stars.

~The Rising~

Posing in the shadow's long hallway,
barren trees, at the doorway of winter--
elegant sentinels, standing tall and proud,
their long arms waving
in November's frigid wind.

On somber days, the sun stolen from the sky,
my heart feels lost, not yet accepting
the sorrow of the season's fate.

And always the shout of crow's anonymous call,
the language of November.

~Gratitude~

*Every morning I give thanks when I wake,
as the pink rays of dawn lift me up,
greet me at my bedroom window.*

*I am grateful, grateful to the wind and sky,
hawk and crow soaring by.*

*Every Spring our wealthy land
gives birth to promise
and crops grow high in fields of splendor.
The angel of gratitude
soars upon wings of serenity,
her heart filled with hope.*

*The golden wealth of Summer,
offering its warm embrace.
The scarlet tears of Fall
passionately follows.*

*On Thanksgiving, the Cornucopia
decorates the festive table.
The sun, a gracious troubadour,
offering tranquility to every heart.*

*And here come chickadees,
sparrows and juncos,
adorning Autumn's sky
with their wings full of blessings.*

*I am grateful, grateful for God's tender grace,
this miracle that is our life.*

~The First Rose~

Everything alive again
Spring at last is here,
The garden oh so magical
As butterflies appear.

A warm breeze moving swiftly
Through the blades of grass,
Winter has departed
A stranger from the past.

White clouds posing on the runway
A dreamy sky of blue,
My heart is so excited
In this world so new.

Baby buds unfolding
Beneath the golden sun,
Happiness fills the soul
And makes the heart feel young.

In her ruby satin gown
So beautiful to see,
Picked by my father's loving hands
Chosen just for me.

Enchanted flowers celebrate
Adorned in lovely bows,
In my father's loving hands
He brings the year's first rose.

~*A Tribute to Our Father*~

Dear Heavenly Father,
Thank you for creating all the beauty in the world.
The trees of summer, the verdant leaves, so exquisite.
I look outside my window
and everything is green.
The trees and always the sky, I treasure.
These images are just a few
of God's summer dreams.
Beautiful clouds, angora white,
posing elegantly in the horizon.
My heart feels joy,
warmed by the sun.
All the tulips, a colorful family.
Glorious cups, confident soldiers standing tall.
Serene and happy being themselves,
filled with gratitude just being alive.
Always the daisies, my favorite flowers.
The purity of their spirits smiling.
Of course the roses, red, yellow, white,
a gift for the most special occasions.
They are angels with the scent of heaven,
alive in their souls.
I thank You Father, creator of life.
We praise You
and give You all the glory.

~Wild Violets~

Here in this patch of violets,
a sliver of white,
a wing of the dove's moon.
The celestial rose wilts
when the last violet is picked,
when the black shawl,
tightly knitted,
is draped over the stars.

~The Truth about This Hour~

Do you understand the song of angels?
Their secret language
the paradise that is you,
and you.

Close your eyes.
Feel the fingers of the wind,
the hand reaching down,
that secret breeze
whispering in your ear.

What is there to question
when you hear that song?
The song of being alive
the melody within.

~Goodbye~

What shall I say again today about you, my love?
What song shall my heart sing,
what song shall my heart sing just for you?

I hold your summer's hand, kiss it tenderly
and take your dying breath
into my own.

There's a charcoal sky at twilight.
For months the fires
have been blazing.

Now fall hovers on the auburn tips of leaves.
I feel the ache of sorrow in my soul
as we say Goodbye.

What song shall my heart sing?
What song shall my heart sing,
just for you?

~A Conversation with an August Night~

Good evening August,
I'm so overjoyed to talk with you upon a night so grand.
In this beautiful theatre
the shadows have taken to the skies.

On stage, the birds last fading notes.
Changing sets,
the crickets entertaining the moment with their lovely song.

The gloaming umbra always friendly,
mysterious characters lasso the darkness.

In the near distance,
the steady droning of a lawn mower.
On life's platform,
I will let it be known my appreciation for the first light.

Off in the horizon,
a bold white jet stream, so quickly fades the vesper.

The morning dove, dressed in formal attire,
is contributing her message to the day's end.
In tune with a distant flute,
harmony of merriment from the voice of angels.

Silhouettes stretch their darkening muscles,
rising to meet the moon
and carry her off into another happy ending.

My poem completed, but alas,
I am unwilling to depart from this somber arena.

They raise their fervor high as the fluttering voice of sparrows.
It takes my breath away once again.

The imprint of a wilting summer dream bids goodnight.
This, another chapter of the twilight chronicles.

~ Always Together~

I remember Laura
first day that I met her,
hiding behind two lonely, hazel eyes.

She had so much to cope with
endured her daily struggles,
in a body extremely compromised.

I remember Thomas
the first time he saw me,
an air of confidence entered the room.

I was struck so kindly
when he spoke to me quite sweetly,
I felt like a rose just beginning to bloom.

Our conversation it was endless
this night very different,
normally our hearts more quiet than this.

But words flowed very freely
pure magic in the air,
the evening ended with a sweet and gentle kiss.

I thought my quest impossible
to meet my knight in shining armor,
but he stood before me with his shield and sword.

My heart beating quickly
ever so quickly,
this true love sent here by our precious Lord.

Always together
we'll always be together,
on earth then in the distant sky.

In the glorious heavens
we'll walk across green meadows,
always together, forever you and I.

~ My Brothers~

This day, the sky painted with the richness
of clouds, a mural of soft brush strokes,
I thrill to the sound of your battle cry.

My beloved crows, I hear you calling,
loud and raucous in April's sky.
Ebony musicians, I love your every note
harmonizing with the choir of all birds.

My brothers, I love your confidence,
never afraid to be heard.
Little generals, commanding land and sky
with a dominant air.

In all seasons, you remain permanent dwellers,
forever loyal to earth and sky, surveying the land
from your post in the birch, the maple, the elm.

I love everything about you dear brothers,
the intensity of your soul
a sentinel perched in the highest branches
an icon of all seasons.

Noble guardian, the echo of your call
can be heard across the world
and forever in my own backyard.

~My Two Angels RyRy and Sandy Madden~

I know two beautiful angels
the Lord blessed me with this gift.
They are the sunshine in my life.
We are injured soldiers,
the sharp edges of who we were
softened now,
but our spirit's light burns brighter.

We are soul sisters,
this sacred kinship,
you bring the strength and the courage
to the flowers of my garden.

Our friendship newly born,
hand in hand in hand,
our travels a similar road
paved with roses.
The symphony of our hearts
gaily dance to.
We are God's children
safe in the cradle of His arms.

~My Onyx Friends~

And behold the crows,
perched right there
upon the edge of June.

You are the signature for all seasons.

I especially love our long chats
together in July.

Onyx are your imperial quills,
the jewels of August.

Your feathers glistening
in sunlight as you soar.

And there you are in September,
wings outstretched.
Drops of oil shimmering in
the last rays of summer.

Always we are the best of friends,
our spirits aglow in the turnstile
of every delicious, vibrant day.

~Writing Angels~

There's a paradise in my mind,
when thoughts are lit by stars.
Hearts excited, kicking up their heels,
dazzling the night's sky.
The lion roars in jubilation,
my heart filled with pride,
as angels whisper thoughts to me
in passionate voices.
My spirit dances,
as words flow easily
from the river of my mind.
I'm showered in rose petals,
my spirit flourishes with so much joy
my heart cannot bear it.
My soul now calm, my purest,
wildest thoughts are yours,
my darling, my love—my poems,
until the ink dries
and the last passionate thought
trembles humbly from my pen.

~Barefoot in Heaven~

When I leave this world,
   I would love for God to
     Take my hand into His own,
       Walk with me to heaven,
         And dance barefoot in the
           Garden of euphoria forever!

~The Heart of Summer~

This is the heart of summer.
This day, this very moment.
My affection belongs to you Oh precious one.
Everyday so exciting,
so many gifts from the heavens above.
Oh sacred one, I must talk of my gratitude
for your many blessings.
The sun, my faithful comrade,
your golden rays a halo above my head,
warming the horizon.
All around me amazing trees
form a canopy of verdant bliss
as the wind whistles through the leaves.
When I turn my head this way, that way,
bouquets of beautiful flowers
perfume the air with loveliness.
From dusk till dawn a song to be heard.
Butterflies whisper to the birds their aerial requests.
"Of course, of course, "the birds sing happily.
The song of angels fills the air,
their tender souls delighted.
Oh sky of God's perfection,
fill me with your beauty.
All the stars twinkle brightly hearing my prayer.
Always the mention of crickets.

~ Kind People ~

*The quick flash of a camera
taking the perfect picture.
Sometimes she felt strong and thought
she could gallop with the wild horses
and mingle with the hungry herd.*

*Eye to eye she would look courageously
into each face, her heart would not quiver,
her words would glisten, like silver rivers
rushing over polished stones.*

*If this dream came true, she could dance among
the stars in another galaxy. If this dream came true,
she would no longer live in alienation
with the few kind people of the world.*

*For a moment, she could drink their wine
and live inside their social caves.
But when the stars begin to fall in the stormy fire,
she will be on the island,
watching the world disappear into the sea,
a leader of a small band of kind people.*

~ In the Present Moment~

In the present moment
February trees
Gaze at me
With gothic beauty
So manicured,
Their tawny limbs.
Another day,
Dressed in gray,
The sky like a lid,
Topping off the horizon.
Ah, this world,
More than lovely,
My spirit ecstatic
Like gentle ocean waves.
The writer's hand,
Freely moves across the page.
Oh, beautiful day,
Spin me a rainbow,
A rainbow of ink,
Sculpturing this day's promise,
As I sit in awe,
In the presence of a
Greater Power.

~ More Than a Job ~

My tears are specks of dust falling. My body is a factory.
My heart is a time clock, you punch in, you punch out.

In the corners of my soul are the shadows of despair.
I am not a bolt to be sorted or a piece of material to be sewn.
I am flesh and blood; my feelings are tender.
Please treat me like a person.

I understand your financial burdens.
I understand your need to survive.

You don't look back at the end of the day. Your wings open
and soar as you fly away.
The prison of my body is the factory where you work.

I am here forever, forever I am here.

About the Author

If someone was to meet Laura Chagnon, they most likely would not believe she is a published poet. Confined to a wheelchair, she has been quadriplegic and legally blind for 35 years. Therefore, she can not write with a pen or use a computer. Her visual challenge prevents Laura from reading her own words. Her short-term memory is greatly hindered as well. This all stems from one incident on her 26th birthday, November 4th, 1989. Laura was the victim of a senseless assault. By the grace of God, she survived and thrived in her challenging world. Five weeks in a coma followed by over three years in speech, physical and occupational rehab facilities was her journey. In 1992, Laura returned to the home of her parents, Wayne and Carole to start a new life. Their unconditional love was the hope that Laura desperately needed.

Ever since she was a teenager, Laura loved writing poetry. She shifted gears by dictating to her caregivers. They would write her words in a thought book then the finished product would be saved on a computer.

In 2014, Laura's door to becoming a published poet swung wide open as she met her friend and publisher, Todd Civin. They collaborated on her first book, "Never Touched a Pen." What a perfect team, fast forward to 2024 "Always Together" is book number twelve. Laura has a work ethic to be envied and shows no signs of slowing down.

Also in 2014, Laura became a motivational speaker by sharing her life story in prisons. With over 200 presentations, she has put hope in the hearts of more than 6,000 inmates.

What a fantastic journey and I'm sure the future holds much more for Laura. She has been linked to her life partner, Tom, for 24 years. But they both are aware it is God who is in control and guides them along. They praise Him every day and give Him all the glory.

Made in the USA
Middletown, DE
23 December 2024